True Love...

D1555844

He came to me with the most wonderful
tenderness. He was afraid and I was afraid, but
there it was, that openness: he was as delicate
and fragile and beautiful as a flower, the
blossom trembling in full bloom....

VICTORIA FREEMAN

He poured so gently and naturally into my life
like batter into a bowl of batter.
Honey into a jar of honey.
The clearest water sinking into sand.

JUSTINE SYDNEY

Your courageous gaiety has inspired me with joy.
Your tender faithfulness has been a rock of
security and comfort. I have felt for you all kinds of
love at once. I have asked much of you and you
have never failed me. You have intensified all
colours, heightened all beauty, deepened all delight.
I love you more than life, my beauty, my wonder.

DUFF COOPER (1890-1954),
TO HIS FUTURE WIFE DIANA, 1918

I need your love as a touchstone of my existence.
It is the sun which breathes life into me.

JULIETTE DROUET, *TO VICTOR HUGO*

When I think of you, it is like thinking of life. You will be the first woman to make the earth glad for me … you are strong and rosy as the gates of Eden. We do not, all of us, not many, perhaps, set out from a sunny paradise of childhood. We are born with our parents in the desert, and yearn for a Canaan. You are like Canaan – you are rich and fruitful and glad and I love you.

D. H. LAWRENCE (1885-1930),
TO LOUISE BURROWS, TO WHOM HE WAS BRIEFLY ENGAGED

...My life, my dear sweet life, my life-light, my all, my goods and chattels, my castles, acres, lawns and vineyards, O sun of my life, sun, moon, and stars, heaven and earth, my past and future, my bride, my girl, my dear friend, my inmost being, my heart-blood, my entrails, star of my eyes, O dearest, what shall I call you?

HEINRICH VON KLEIST (1777-1811),
TO ADOLFINE HENRIETTE VOGEL

Love must be learned, and learned again
and again; there is no end to it.

KATHERINE ANN PORTER (1890-1980)

He is not a lover who does not love forever.

EURIPIDES (484-406 B.C.)

Many waters cannot quench love, neither
can the floods drown it.

SONG OF SOLOMON 8:7

The heart that loves is always young.

GREEK PROVERB

The countless generations
Like Autumn leaves go by:
Love only is eternal,
Love only does not die …

HARRY KEMP,
FROM *"THE PASSING FLOWER"*

Love is an act of endless forgiveness.

PETER USTINOV, b.1921

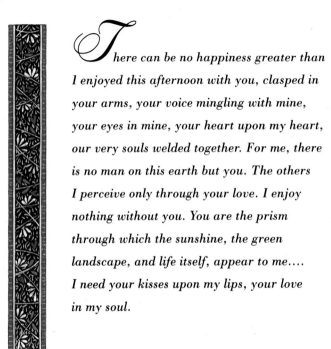

There can be no happiness greater than I enjoyed this afternoon with you, clasped in your arms, your voice mingling with mine, your eyes in mine, your heart upon my heart, our very souls welded together. For me, there is no man on this earth but you. The others I perceive only through your love. I enjoy nothing without you. You are the prism through which the sunshine, the green landscape, and life itself, appear to me.... I need your kisses upon my lips, your love in my soul.

JULIETTE DROUET, *TO VICTOR HUGO*

Love gives us in a moment what we can hardly
attain by effort after years of toil.

S.W. VON GOETHE (1749-1832)

In fact, though their acquaintance had been so
short, they had guessed, as always happens
between lovers, everything of any importance
about each other in two seconds at the
utmost....

VIRGINIA WOOLF (1882-1941)

To love is the great Amulet that makes this
world a garden.

ROBERT LOUIS STEVENSON (1850-1894)

My heart is like a singing bird …
Because the birthday of my life
Is come, my love is come to me.

CHRISTINA ROSSETTI (1830-1894)

No cord or cable can draw so forcibly, or bind
so fast, as love can do with a single thread.

ROBERT BURTON (1577-1640)

… You were made perfectly to be loved –
and surely I have loved you,
in the idea of you, my whole life long.

ELIZABETH BARRETT (1806-1861),
TO HER FUTURE HUSBAND ROBERT BROWNING

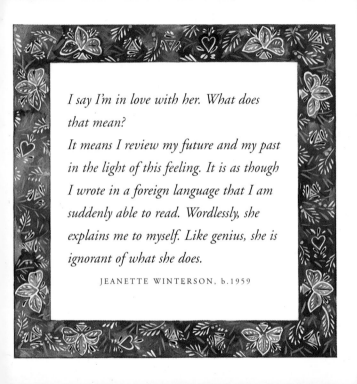

I say I'm in love with her. What does
that mean?
It means I review my future and my past
in the light of this feeling. It is as though
I wrote in a foreign language that I am
suddenly able to read. Wordlessly, she
explains me to myself. Like genius, she is
ignorant of what she does.

JEANETTE WINTERSON, b.1959

… falling in love … is a simultaneous firing
of two spirits engaged in the autonomous act
of growing up. And the sensation
is of something having noiselessly
exploded inside each of them.

LAWRENCE DURRELL (1912-1990)

You have absorb'd me. I have a sensation at the
present moment as though I was dissolving.

JOHN KEATS (1795-1821),
TO FANNY BRAWNE

O lyric love, half angel and half bird,
And all a wonder and a wild desire!

ROBERT BROWNING (1812-1889)

"I can make you happy,"

said he…. "And at

home by the fire,

whenever you look up,

there I shall be –

and whenever I look up,

there will be you."

THOMAS HARDY (1840-1928),
FROM "FAR FROM THE
MADDING CROWD"

"My well-beloved is mine and I am his." Love was their banqueting-house, love was their wine, love was their ensign; love was his invitings, love was her faintings; love was his apples, love was her comforts; love was his embracings, love was her refreshing; love made him see her, love made her seek him; love made him wed her, love made her follow him; … Love bred our fellowship, let love continue it, and love shall increase it until death dissolve it.

JOHN WINTHROP (1588-1649),
FIRST GOVERNOR OF
THE MASSACHUSETTS BAY COLONY,
TO HIS FIANCÉE

Love is supposed to start with bells ringing and go downhill from there. But it was the opposite for me. There's an intense connection between us, and as we stayed together, the bells rang louder.

LISA NIEMI

That is true love which always and forever remains the same, whether one grants it everything or denies it everything.

S. W. VON GOETHE (1749-1832)

To-day a new sun rises for me; everything lives, everything is animated, everything seems to speak to me of my passion, everything invites me to cherish it. The fire consuming me gives to my heart, to all the faculties of my soul, a resilience, an activity which is diffused through all my affections. Since I loved you, my friends are dearer to me; I love myself more; ... the sounds of my lute seem to me more moving, my voices more harmonious.

NINON DE L'ENCLOS,
TO THE MARQUIS DE SÉVIGNY IN THE 1600s

$\mathcal{M}$y door has not been opened once today, but what my heart palpitated. There were moments when I feared to hear your voice, and then I was disconsolate that it was not your voice. So many contradictions, so many contrary movements are true, and can be explained in three words: I LOVE YOU.

JULIE DE L'ESPINASSE,
*TO COMTE HIPPOLYTE
DE GUIBERT, 1774*

So dear I love him that with him all deaths I could endure, without him live no life.

JOHN MILTON (1608-1674)

Only three things are infinite: the sky in its stars, the sea in its drops of water, and the heart in its tears.

GUSTAVE FLAUBERT (1821-1880)

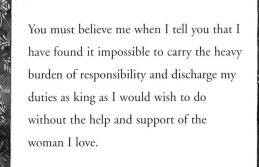

You must believe me when I tell you that I have found it impossible to carry the heavy burden of responsibility and discharge my duties as king as I would wish to do without the help and support of the woman I love.

EDWARD VIII (1894-1972),
WHEN HE GAVE UP THE THRONE
OF THE UNITED KINGDOM
TO MARRY WALLIS SIMPSON

How am I to tell you that I am intoxicated with the faintest odour of you, that, had I possessed you a thousand times, you would see me still more intoxicated, because there would be hope and memory where there is as yet only hope.

HONORÉ DE BALZAC (1799-1859),
*TO HIS FUTURE WIFE MADAME
EVELINE HANSKA*

To love is also good, for love is difficult.
For one human being to love another is
perhaps the most difficult task of all, the
epitome, the ultimate test. It is that
striving for which all other striving is
merely preparation.

RANIER MARIA RILKE (1875-1926)

For finally, we are as we love. It is love
that measures our stature.

WILLIAM SLOANE COFFIN

The truth [is] that there is only one terminal dignity – love. And the story of a love is not important – what is important is that one is capable of love. It is perhaps the only glimpse we are permitted of eternity.

HELEN HAYES

Love alone is capable of uniting human beings in such a way as to complete and fulfil them, for it alone takes them and joins them by what is deepest in themselves.

PIÉRRE TEILHARD DE CHARDIN

Oh, God! ... for two days, I have been asking myself every moment if such happiness is not a dream. It seems to me that what I feel is not of earth. I cannot yet comprehend this cloudless heaven.

VICTOR HUGO (1802-1885),
TO ADÈLE FOUCHER

There is nothing holier, in this life of ours, than the first consciousness of love – the first fluttering of its silken wings.

HENRY WADSWORTH LONGFELLOW
(1807-1882)

I bless you.
I kiss & caress every tenderly
beloved place & gaze into your deep,
sweet eyes which long ago conquered
me completely.
Love ever grows.

TSARITSA ALEXANDRA *(1872-1918)*,
TO TSAR NICHOLAS II OF RUSSIA

In loving you, I love the best the
world has to give.

ROBERT SCHUMANN (1810-1956),
TO HIS FUTURE WIFE CLARA WIECK

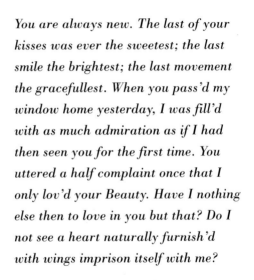

You are always new. The last of your kisses was ever the sweetest; the last smile the brightest; the last movement the gracefullest. When you pass'd my window home yesterday, I was fill'd with as much admiration as if I had then seen you for the first time. You uttered a half complaint once that I only lov'd your Beauty. Have I nothing else then to love in you but that? Do I not see a heart naturally furnish'd with wings imprison itself with me?

JOHN KEATS (1795-1821),
TO FANNY BRAWNE

It is that moment that divides
the intoxication of Life from the
awakening. It is the first flame
that lights up the inner domain
of the heart. It is the first magic
note plucked on the silver string
of the heart....

KAHLIL GIBRAN (1883-1931)

Love can never more grow old,
Locks may lose their brown and gold,
Cheeks may fade and hollow grow,
But the hearts that love will know
Never winter's frost and chill,
Summer's warmth is in them still.

EBEN EUGENE REXFORD

Love bears all things, believes all things,
hopes all things, endures all things.
Love never ends.

1 CORINTHIANS 13:7

Love keeps the cold out better
than a cloak.

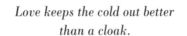

HENRY WADSWORTH LONGFELLOW
(1807-1882)

Love is like the measles; we all have
to go through it.

JEROME K. JEROME (1859-1927)

Love may not make the world go
round, but I must admit that it makes
the ride worthwhile.

SEAN CONNERY, b.1930

What thing is love? for, well I wot,
love is a thing.
It is a prick, it is a sting,
It is a pretty pretty thing;
It is a fire, it is a coal,
Whose flame creeps in at every hole;
And as my wit doth best devise,
Love's dwelling is in ladies' eyes:
From whence do glance love's piercing darts
That make such holes into our hearts;

GEORGE PEELE (1558-1597),
FROM *"WHAT THING IS LOVE?"*

She half enclosed me with her arms,
She pressed me with a meek embrace;
And bending back her head, looked up,
And gazed upon my face.
'Twas partly love, and partly fear,
And partly 'twas a bashful art,
That I might rather feel, than see,
The swelling of her heart.

SAMUEL TAYLOR COLERIDGE (1772-1834)

Infatuation is when you think that he's as sexy as
Robert Redford, as smart as Henry Kissinger, as
noble as Ralph Nader, as funny as Woody Allen,
and as athletic as Jimmy Connors. Love is when
you realize that he's as sexy as Woody Allen, as
smart as Jimmy Connors, as funny as Ralph Nader,
as athletic as Henry Kissinger and nothing like
Robert Redford – but you'll take him anyway.

JUDITH VIORST, b.1935

My darling, dear, delightful Ringo, could you please
send me something of yours? Anything, a lock of
hair, a thread from your coat, a smoked cigarette,
a button from your shirt, a piece of old toast,
or a bristle from your toothbrush. I would
treasure it forever.

MARY L., TO BEATLE, RINGO STARR

In dreams and in love there are no impossibilities.

JANUS ARONY

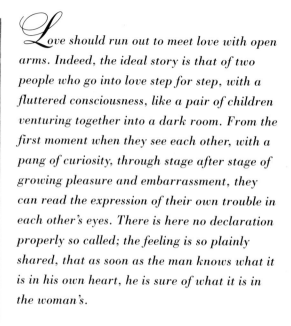

Love should run out to meet love with open arms. Indeed, the ideal story is that of two people who go into love step for step, with a fluttered consciousness, like a pair of children venturing together into a dark room. From the first moment when they see each other, with a pang of curiosity, through stage after stage of growing pleasure and embarrassment, they can read the expression of their own trouble in each other's eyes. There is here no declaration properly so called; the feeling is so plainly shared, that as soon as the man knows what it is in his own heart, he is sure of what it is in the woman's.

ROBERT LOUIS STEVENSON (1850-1894),
FROM *"VIRGINIBUS PUERISQUE"*

A something in your eyes, and voice, you possess
in a degree more persuasive than any woman I
ever saw, read, or heard of ... that bewitching
sort of nameless excellence.

LAURENCE STERNE (1713-1768)

I love thee to the depth and breadth and height
My soul can reach....

ELIZABETH BARRETT BROWNING (1806-1861)

… everything you do souses me, terrifies
me, tortures me, elates me, everything you
do is perfect.

PAUL ELUARD (PAUL-EUGÉNE GRINDEL),
TO HIS WIFE ELENA DMITRIEVNA DIAKONOVA

I think you are good, gifted, lovely: a fervent, a
solemn passion is conceived in my heart; it leans
to you, draws you to my centre and spring of life,
wraps my existence about you – and, kindling in
pure, powerful flame, fuses you and me in one.

CHARLOTTE BRONTË (1816-1855),
FROM *"JANE EYRE"*

… it will bloom always fairer, fresher, more gracious, because it is a true love, and because genuine love is ever increasing. It is a beautiful plant growing from year to year in the heart, ever extending its palms and branches, doubling every season its glorious clusters and perfumes; and, my dear life, tell me, repeat to me always, that nothing will bruise its bark or its delicate leaves, that it will grow larger in both our hearts, loved, free, watched over, like a life within our life …

HONORÉ DE BALZAC (1799-1859),
TO HIS FUTURE WIFE MADAME EVELINA HANSKA

Never forget that the most powerful force
on earth is Love.

NELSON ROCKERFELLER (1908-1979)

Love is love's reward.

JOHN DRYDEN (1631-1700)

Love is the master key that opens the gates
of happiness.

OLIVER WENDELL HOLMES (1809-1894)

Love is, above all, the gift of oneself.

JEAN ANOUILH (1910-1987)

Love is not a union merely between two
creatures – it is a union between two spirits.

FREDERICK W. ROBERTSON (1816-1853)

Love is the heart's immortal thirst
to be completely known and all forgiven.

HENRY VAN DYKE (1852-1933)

Love is never having to say you're sorry.

ERICH SEGAL, b.1937

... Under the summer roses,
When the fragrant crimson
Lurks in the dusk
Of the wild red leaves,
Love, with little hands,
Comes and touches you
With a thousand memories,
And asks you
Beautiful, unanswerable questions.

CARL SANDBURG (1878-1967)

I do love you … as the dew loves the flowers; as the birds love the sunshine; as the wavelets love the breeze; as mothers love their firstborn; as memory loves old faces; as the yearning tides love the moon; as angels love the pure in heart.

MARK TWAIN (1835-1910)

I love you soulfully and bodyfully, properly and improperly, every way that a woman can be loved.

GEORGE BERNARD SHAW (1856-1950),
TO ELLEN TERRY

True love is but a humble
    low-born thing,
And hath its food served
    up in earthen ware;
It is a thing to walk with,
    hand in hand,
Through the every-dayness
    of this work-day world.

JAMES RUSSELL LOWELL
(1819-1892)

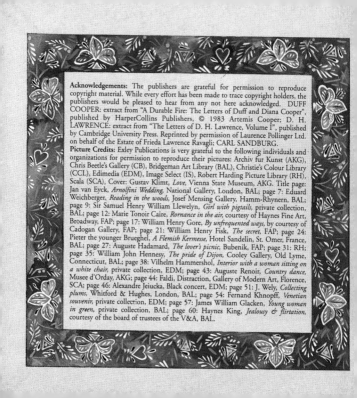

Acknowledgements: The publishers are grateful for permission to reproduce copyright material. While every effort has been made to trace copyright holders, the publishers would be pleased to hear from any not here acknowledged. DUFF COOPER: extract from "A Durable Fire: The Letters of Duff and Diana Cooper", published by HarperCollins Publishers, © 1983 Artemis Cooper; D. H. LAWRENCE: extract from "The Letters of D. H. Lawrence, Volume I", published by Cambridge University Press. Reprinted by permission of Laurence Pollinger Ltd. on behalf of the Estate of Frieda Lawrence Ravagli; CARL SANDBURG.

Picture Credits: Exley Publications is very grateful to the following individuals and organizations for permission to reproduce their pictures: Archiv fur Kunst (AKG), Chris Beetle's Gallery (CB), Bridgeman Art Library (BAL), Christie's Colour Library (CCL), Edimedia (EDM), Image Select (IS), Robert Harding Picture Library (RH), Scala (SCA), Cover: Gustav Klimt, *Love*, Vienna State Museum, AKG. Title page: Jan van Eyck, *Arnolfini Wedding*, National Gallery, London, BAL; page 7: Eduard Weichberger, *Reading in the woods*, Josef Mensing Gallery, Hamm-Rhynern, BAL; page 9: Sir Samuel Henry William Llewelyn, *Girl with pigtails*, private collection, BAL; page 12: Marie Tonoir Caire, *Rormance in the air*, courtesy of Haynes Fine Art, Broadway, FAP; page 17: William Henry Gore, *By unfrequented ways*, by courtesy of Cadogan Gallery, FAP; page 21: William Henry Fisk, *The secret*, FAP; page 24: Pieter the younger Brueghel, *A Flemish Kermesse*, Hotel Sandelin, St. Omer, France, BAL; page 27: Auguste Hadamard, *The lover's picnic*, Bubenik, FAP; page 31: RH; page 35: William John Hennesy, *The pride of Dijon*, Cooley Gallery, Old Lyme, Connecticut, BAL; page 38: Vilhelm Hammershol, *Interior with a woman sitting on a white chair*, private collection, EDM; page 43: Auguste Renoir, *Country dance*, Musee d'Orday, AKG; page 44: Faldi, *Distraction*, Gallery of Modern Art, Florence, SCA; page 46: Alexandre Jeiucka, *Black concert*, EDM; page 51: J. Wely, *Collecting plums*, Whitford & Hughes, London, BAL; page 54: Fernand Khnopff, *Venetian souvenir*, private collection, EDM; page 57: James William Glacken, *Young woman in green*, private collection, BAL; page 60: Haynes King, *Jealousy & flirtation*, courtesy of the board of trustees of the V&A, BAL.